Sports Figures

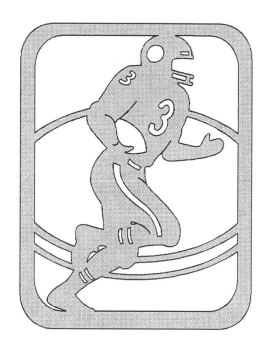

Patrick Spielman
& Brian Dahlen

STERLING PUBLISHING CO., INC.
NEW YORK

Acknowledgment

Much gratitude and appreciation are expressed to Julie Kiehnau, our typist, who also expertly cut out the projects pictured on the cover.

Library of Congress Cataloging-in-Publication Data

Spielman, Patrick E.
    Sports figures / by Patrick Spielman and Brian Dahlen.
        p.   cm. — (Woodworker's pattern library series)
    Includes index.
    ISBN 0-8069-0485-2
        1. Jig saws.   2. Woodwork—Patterns.   3. Sports in art.
    4. Silhouettes.   I. Dahlen, Brian.   II. Title.   III. Series.
    TT186.S676   1994
    745.51—dc20   93-48073
                                                   CIP

Edited by Rodman Neumann

10   9   8   7   6   5   4   3   2   1

Published by Sterling Publishing Company, Inc.
387 Park Avenue South, New York, N.Y. 10016
© 1994 by Patrick Spielman & Brian Dahlen
Distributed in Canada by Sterling Publishing
% Canadian Manda Group, P.O. Box 920, Station U
Toronto, Ontario, Canada M8Z 5P9
Distributed in Great Britain and Europe by Cassell PLC
Villiers House, 41/47 Strand, London WC2N 5JE, England
Distributed in Australia by Capricorn Link (Australia) Pty Ltd.
P.O. Box 6651, Baulkham Hills, Business Centre, NSW 2153, Australia
Manufactured in the United States of America
All rights reserved
ISBN 0-8069-0485-2

Contents

Metric Conversion

Inches	MM	CM	Inches	CM	Inches	CM
⅛	3	0.3	9	22.9	30	76.2
¼	6	0.6	10	25.4	31	78.7
⅜	10	1.0	11	27.9	32	81.3
½	13	1.3	12	30.5	33	83.8
⅝	16	1.6	13	33.0	34	86.4
¾	19	1.9	14	35.6	35	88.9
⅞	22	2.2	15	38.1	36	91.4
1	25	2.5	16	40.6	37	94.0
1¼	32	3.2	17	43.2	38	96.5
1½	38	3.8	18	45.7	39	99.1
1¾	44	4.4	19	48.3	40	101.6
2	51	5.1	20	50.8	41	104.1
2½	64	6.4	21	53.3	42	106.7
3	76	7.6	22	55.9	43	109.2
3½	89	8.9	23	58.4	44	111.8
4	102	10.2	24	61.0	45	114.3
4½	114	11.4	25	63.5	46	116.8
5	127	12.7	26	66.0	47	119.4
6	152	15.2	27	68.6	48	121.9
7	178	17.8	28	71.1	49	124.5
8	203	20.3	29	73.7	50	127.0

Inches to Millimetres and Centimetres
MM—millimetres   CM—centimetres

Preface

This book of sports images for scroll-sawing enthusiasts features over 125 patterns in 34 categories of sporting activities. The pattern designs can be incorporated into functional projects such as sign ornamentations, pegboards, tie and key racks, shelves, and as decorative overlays on boxes, cabinets, clocks, and furniture. Some silhouette patterns are intended only for wall or window decorations. Silhouette pattern projects can be enhanced by attaching thin backers of contrasting colors or using mirrored plastic, which creates a very stunning effect. In many cases the primary design element of a silhouette can be extracted from the surrounding frame and used for other applications.

We encourage you to get the most out of these patterns by considering all of their possibilities for use. These ideas, together with the further possibilities created when you enlarge or reduce the patterns, provide many more potential projects than a simple look at the patterns would indicate.

Because office photocopiers are now so accessible to almost everyone, we've included some tips on how to use them quickly and efficiently to size a pattern or project to any dimension desired. Consequently, you will be able quickly to custom-size a pattern or design a pattern to serve your own needs. Newer photocopy machines are capable of enlarging any original from this book to any size up to 200 percent, in one-percent increments. And you can get even greater enlargements by simply enlarging an already enlarged copy.

Patrick Spielman
and Brian Dahlen

Basic Tips

The patterns and project ideas in this book are essentially fast, easy, and fun to create. Making these cutouts requires no special equipment other than a scroll saw and a drill to make holes for sawing inside openings. Advanced woodworking skills are not required, and anyone beyond the age of eight or nine can learn the fun of scroll sawing and soon be making projects for him- or herself or as gifts. The scroll saw is the easiest woodworking machine to use and it is much safer than all other power tools. If scroll sawing is new for you, we recommend *Scroll Saw Basics* (see page 125); this book provides essential instructions for scroll saws and how to use them to make basic cuts.

Sizing Patterns with a Photocopier

Most communities have photocopiers available with enlarging capabilities; they're found in public libraries, banks, and schools. Print shops and specialized businesses ("copy shops") are found in most areas. Check the business index of your telephone directory under the headings "photocopying" or "copying" for the nearest business specializing in this service. Having a copy made is quick, convenient, and far more expedient and accurate than other old-fashioned ways of copying or enlarging patterns that used the squared grid system or pantograph tracings.

Enlarging with a Proportional Scale

Better-quality photocopiers enlarge or reduce pattern sizes in one-percent increments. Typically, they can enlarge up to 200 percent of the original where the original size is referred to as 100 percent. A proportional scale is an inexpensive circular device that allows you to determine the exact percentage of enlargement or reduction needed to produce a specific-sized pattern. The photocopier is then set to that percentage. The scale is very easy to use; all the little numbers and divisions make it look much more complicated than it really is. This device is simply two rotating discs with numbers and scale divisions around their perimeters joined by a common pivot. Align the number or dimension you have on the inner disc with the dimension you want on the outer disc. The exact percentage to set the copy machine can then be read in the opening directly below the arrow.

An inexpensive proportional scale such as this makes enlarging or reducing patterns to a specific size with a photocopy machine quick and precise.

To see how helpful this tool is, and how easy it actually is to use, follow the steps illustrated here, which show a typical enlargement application. This process eliminates the guesswork and trial-and-error methods from the sizing process. This process also saves paper and money spent on wasted copies. Proportional scales are found in art, graphics, and printing-supply stores. Check the business section of your telephone directory to locate a source for one of these helpful devices.

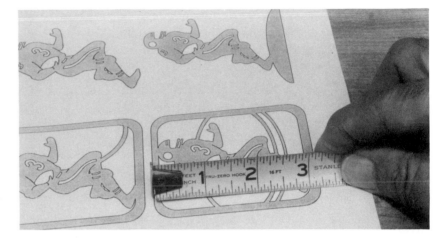

Here's a typical problem example: the objective is to enlarge a pattern from its given size of 3³/₁₆ inches overall to exactly 5³/₄ inches.

Simply line up the 3³/₁₆-inch marker of the inner disc to the 5³/₄-inch marker on the outer disc. Now read the exact percentage required to set the copy machine to get an enlarged copy of the desired size. In this example you'll obtain a 5³/₄-inch pattern when the original is enlarged 180 percent.

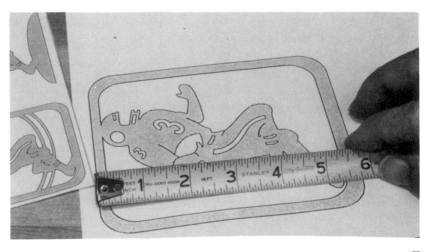

The enlarged copy of the pattern measures exactly 5³/₄ inches overall, as desired.

7

Wood Material and Thickness

A number of patterns will result in very fragile cutouts if sawn from solid wood. Notice the example of the golfer illustrated. In such cases a good grade of plywood such as Baltic birch or other hardwood plywood is recommended rather than solid wood, because of its inherent strength advantage. Many of the fretted silhouette patterns are best sawn from thin plywoods unless they are to be used as overlays and glued to solid backers. The best thickness is a matter of choice, availability, and functional need for the intended end use.

Generally, thin plywood, ¼ inch or less, is satisfactory for some of the hanging projects with ornate fret-type cutouts.

Transferring Patterns to the Wood

Transferring patterns to material for sawing can certainly be done in traditional ways, such as tracing with copy papers (carbon or graphite). However, the new, faster techniques involve: (1) copying the pattern directly from the book on an office-quality copy machine, at which time it can be enlarged or reduced as desired, (2) scissor-cutting the pattern to a rough size, (3) coating the back of the pattern with a very light mist of special spray adhesive, and (4) simply hand-pressing

Delicate designs such as this happy golfer are best sawn from plywood. Solid wood would have areas of very fragile "short grain," regardless of how the pattern is positioned on the wood.

Scissor-cutting a photocopy of the pattern to a rough size.

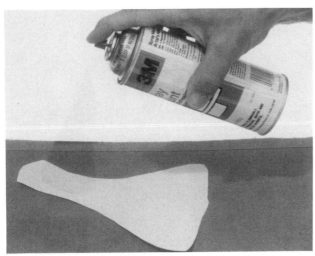

Using an aerosol temporary-bonding adhesive to coat the back of the pattern very lightly. A piece of cardboard catches the excess spray.

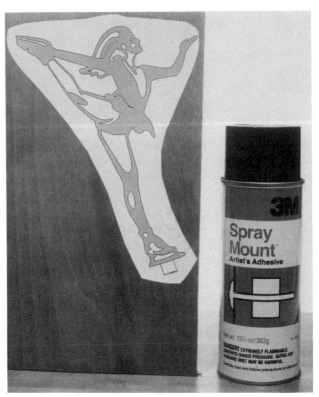

A photocopy of the pattern applied directly to the workpiece ready for scroll-sawing.

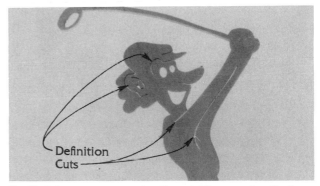

Definition cuts are single-width saw kerfs that originate entirely within the design itself or are cut by sawing inward from the outside edge.

the paper pattern copy directly onto the workpiece. Temporary bonding spray adhesives are available from craft shops and mail-order sources. One kind we use is 3-M's Scotch Brand Spray Mount Adhesive, but other brands work equally well. Some craftspeople prefer using a brush-on application of rubber cement for securing patterns to the workpiece.

Test the adhesive on scrap first, before using. To use the spray adhesive, simply spray a very light mist onto the back of the pattern copy—do not spray it on the wood. Wait 10–30 seconds, and press the pattern onto the workpiece. It should maintain contact during sawing. After all the cutting is completed, the paper pattern should peel very easily and cleanly from the workpiece without effort. Should the pattern be difficult to remove because too much adhesive was used, simply wipe the top of the pattern with a rag that has been slightly dampened in solvent.

Definition Cuts

This is a sawing technique specified on many patterns to make them appear more realistic and detailed. The process involves making a single kerf or interior saw cut through the work to represent a certain feature or effect. Only pinless-

type saw blades can effectively be used for making interior single-line definition cuts. This age-old fretwork technique of making single-line cuts was widely used by scroll sawyers over a hundred years ago. Definition cut lines can originate entirely within the design itself or be cut by sawing inward from the outside edge.

Normally, this work is done with fine, thin blades, but the actual size used depends on the material thickness and the character of the line being cut. Interior veining is most effective when the blade entry hole is barely large enough to permit the blade to be threaded through the work piece. A 3/64-inch-diameter hole will allow the use of a No. 4 scroll/fretsaw blade. A 1/32-inch-diameter hole allows a No. 2 blade. If the material is very thin, try using a sharp knife to make a very narrow, undetectable slit for blade entry.

Scroll-Sawing Tip: Sharpen the end of the blade to a point so that it can be forced into a hole that is smaller than the usual size, to make the blade threading area almost totally undetectable.

Surface detailing lines can also be applied with a woodburning tool. Painted or sealed wood can be lined with ink or soft-tipped felt markers. These methods are especially advantageous when using scroll saws that carry pin-type blades.

Stack-Sawing

Stack-sawing is a basic production technique that should not be overlooked whenever a quantity of the same cutout is required. Stack- or plural-cutting involves sawing two or more layers of material at the same time. Very thin plywood can be stacked to as many as 12 or more layers and cut all at once. Sometimes scroll sawyers will use a cheap, low-grade material as a bottom layer to prevent saw blade tear-out or feathering from occurring on the bottom or exit side of the project itself. Layers can be held together in various ways while they are sawn, including nailing or tacking, spot-gluing in the waste areas, and using double-faced tape.

A segmented overlay project sawn from 1/4-inch-thick material. The edges of every part or segment are rounded over (about 3/16-inch radius), sanded, painted, and glued to a thin-framed panel. Other segmentation project patterns are given on pages 35 and 57.

A close-up look at the segmented racing car plaque. Note how the rounded edges of each segment or part create an interesting shadow and a three-dimensional effect. Water-based acrylic paints were used to color the individual pieces before assembly.

Patterns

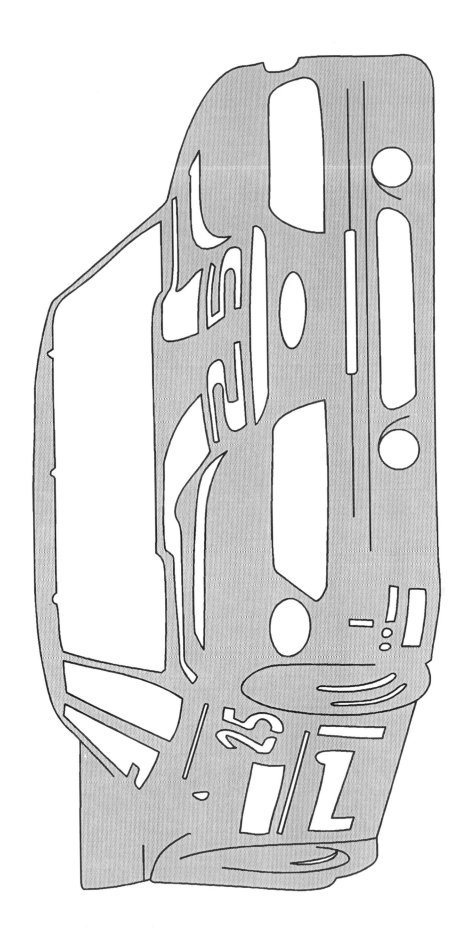

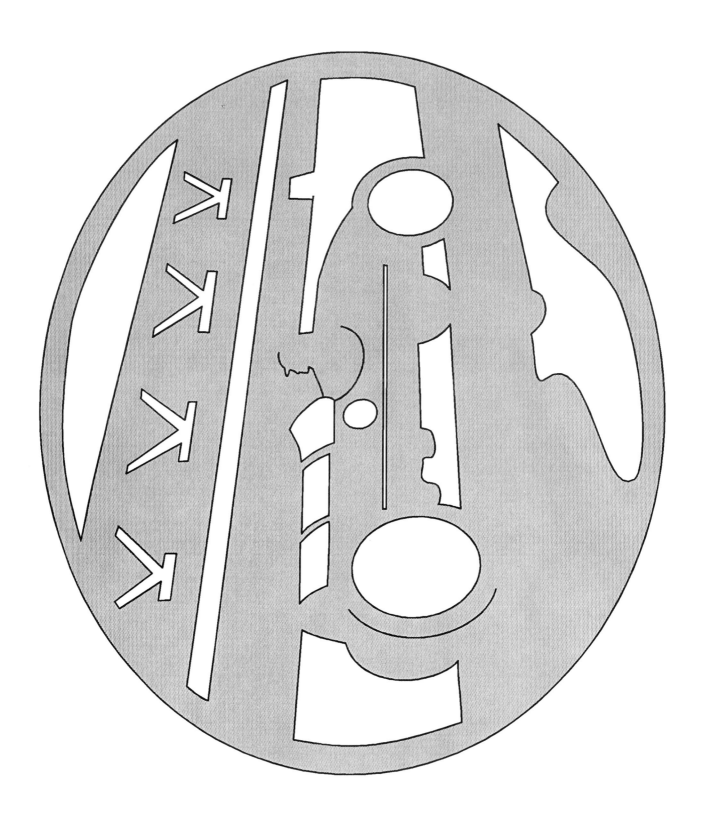

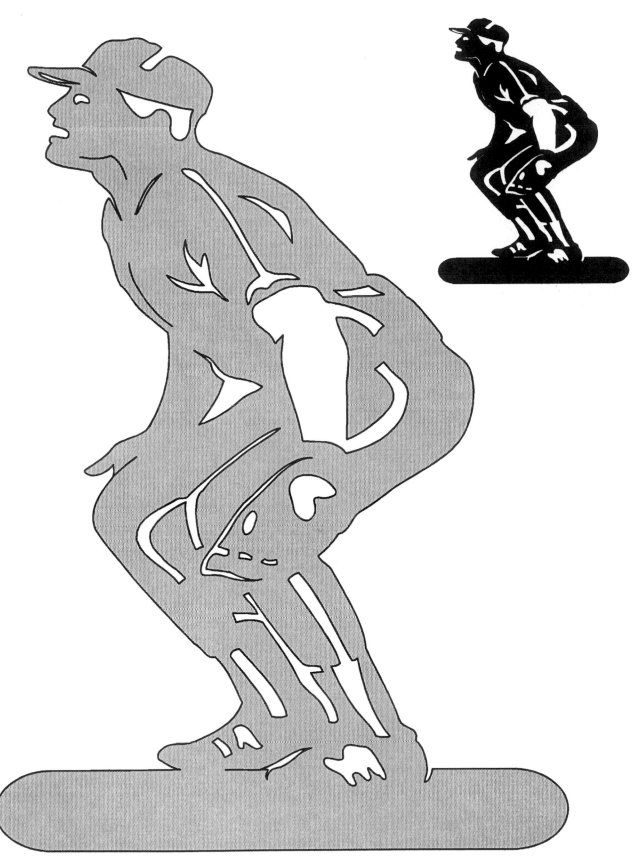

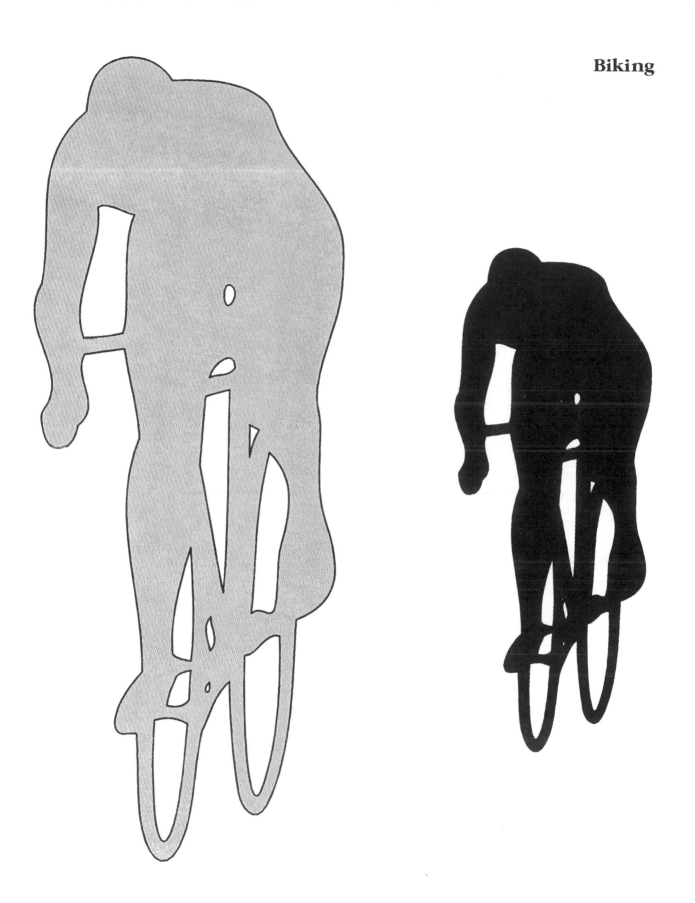

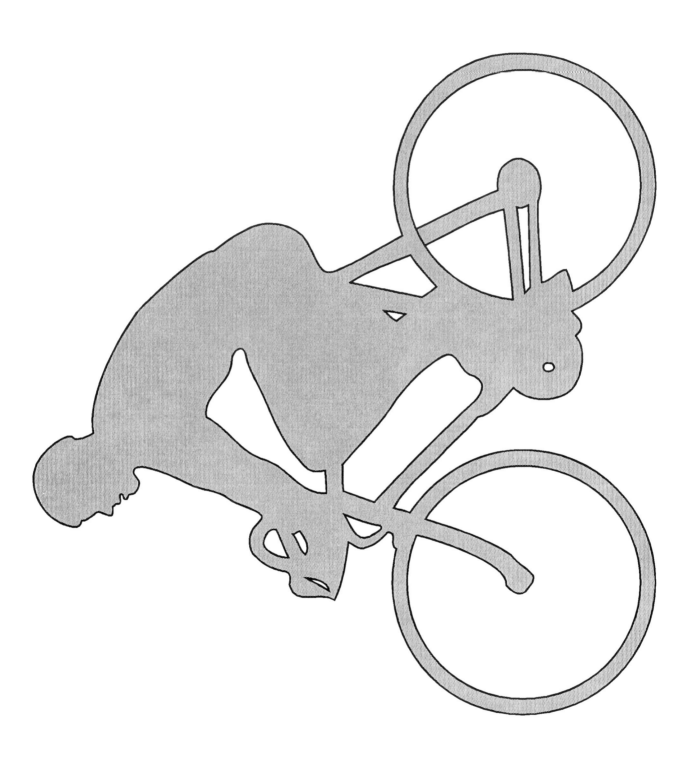

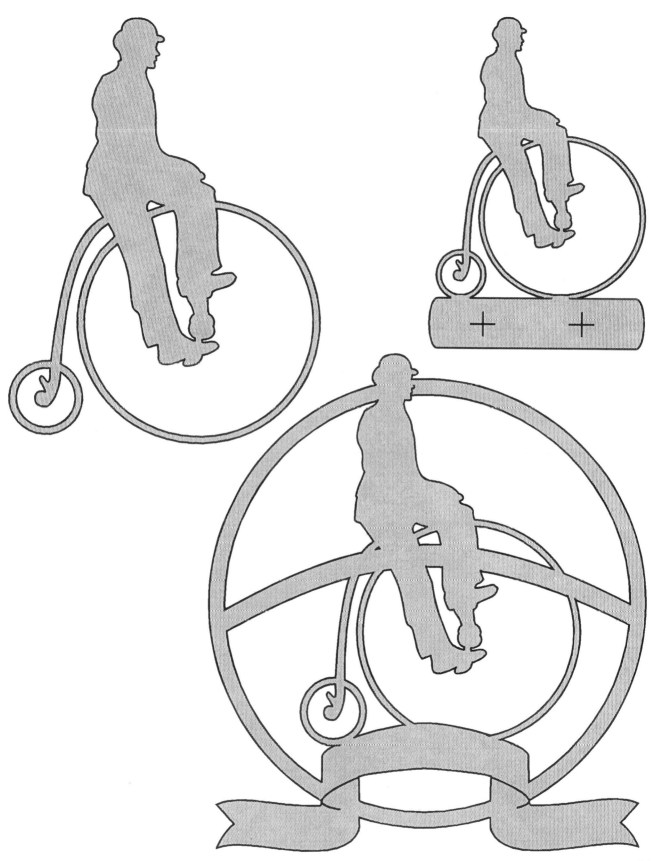

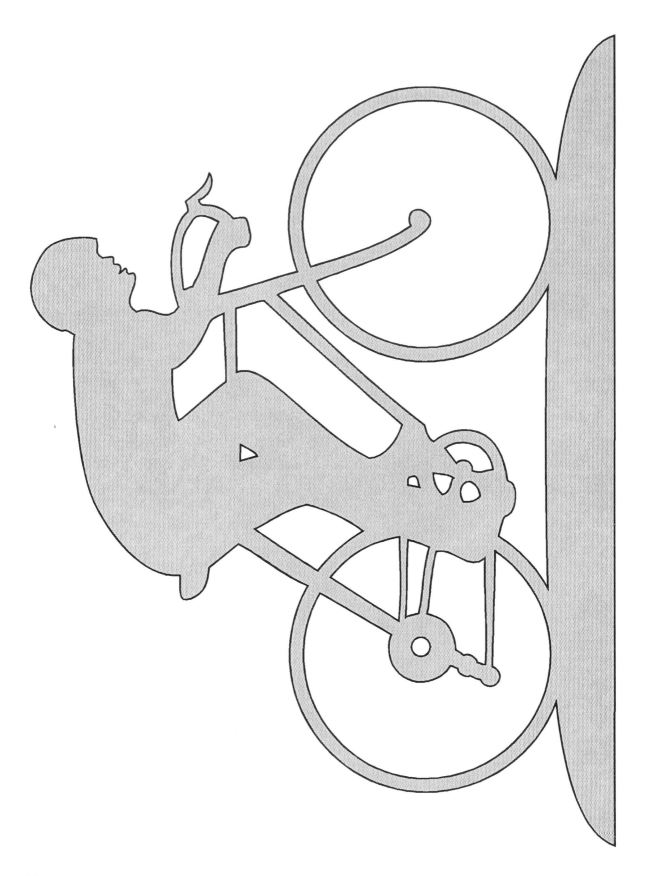

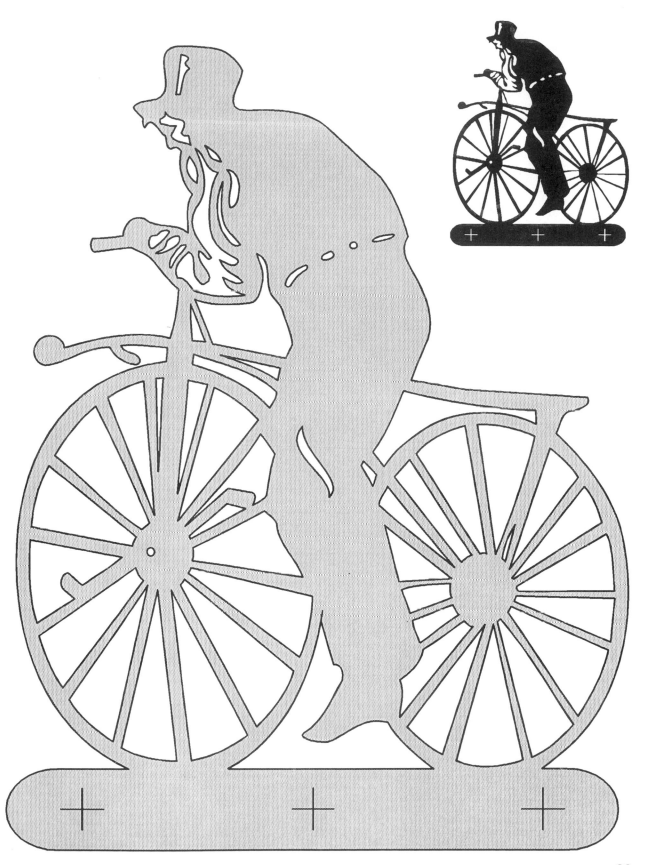

Bowling

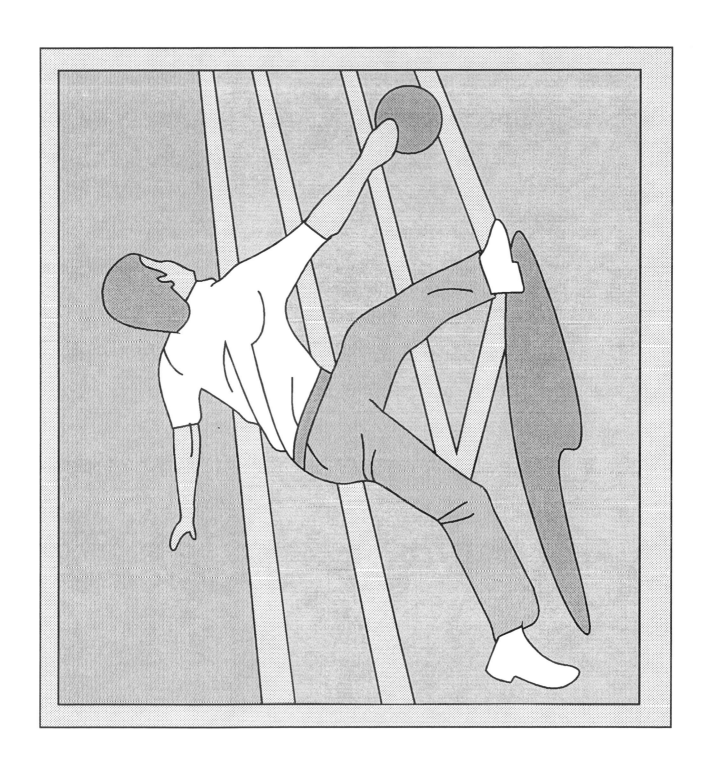

Boxing

Darts

38

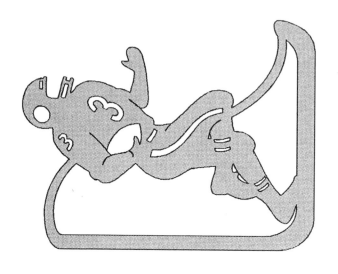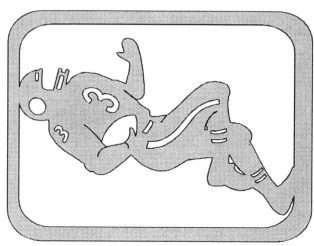

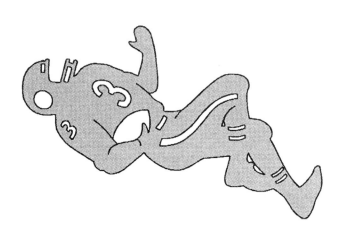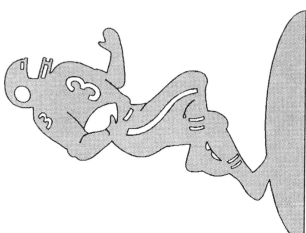

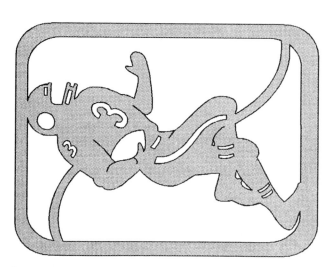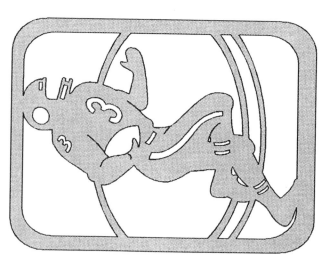

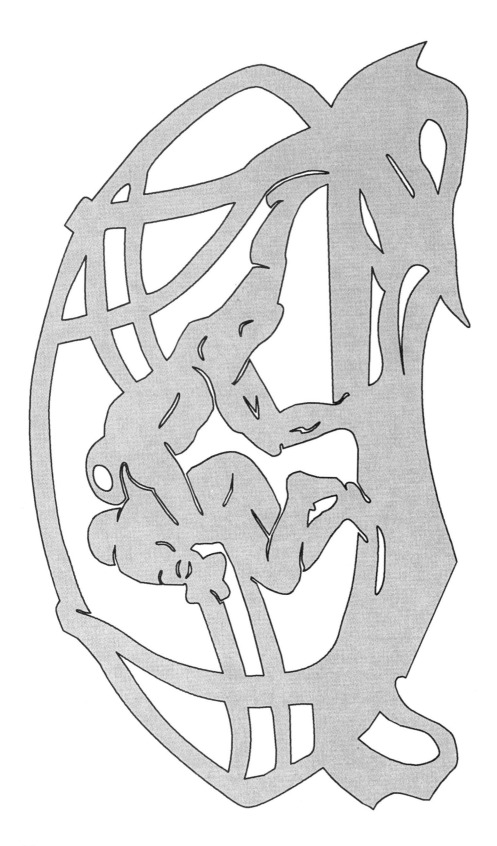

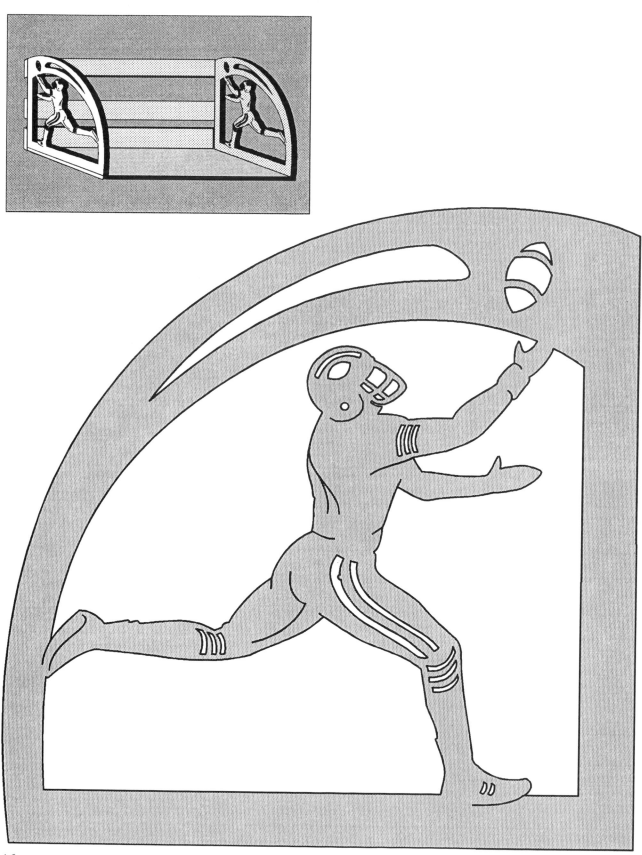

49

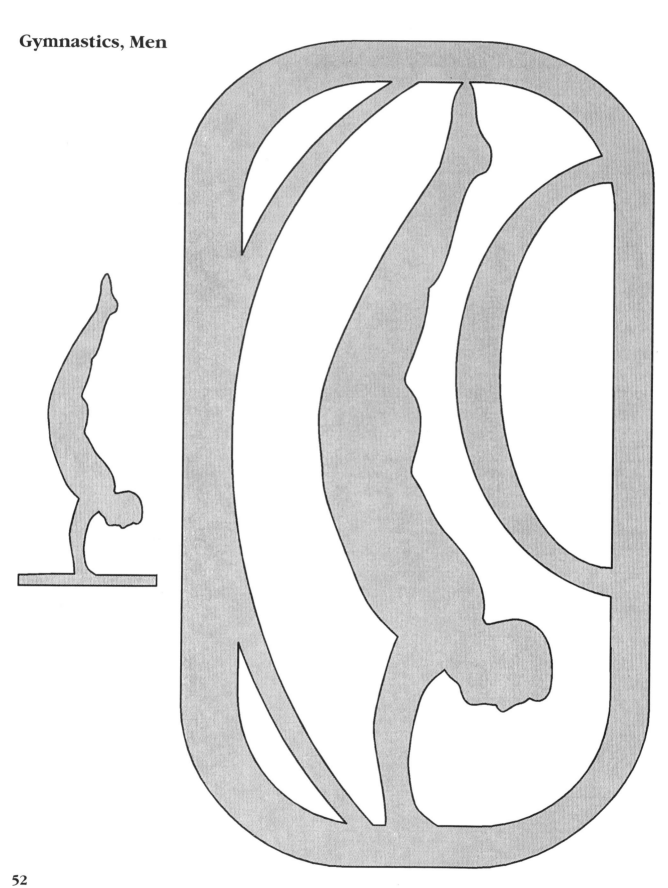

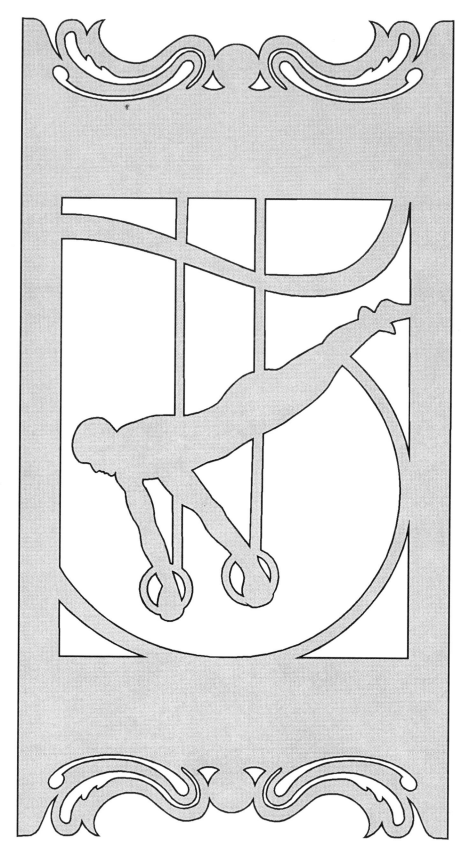

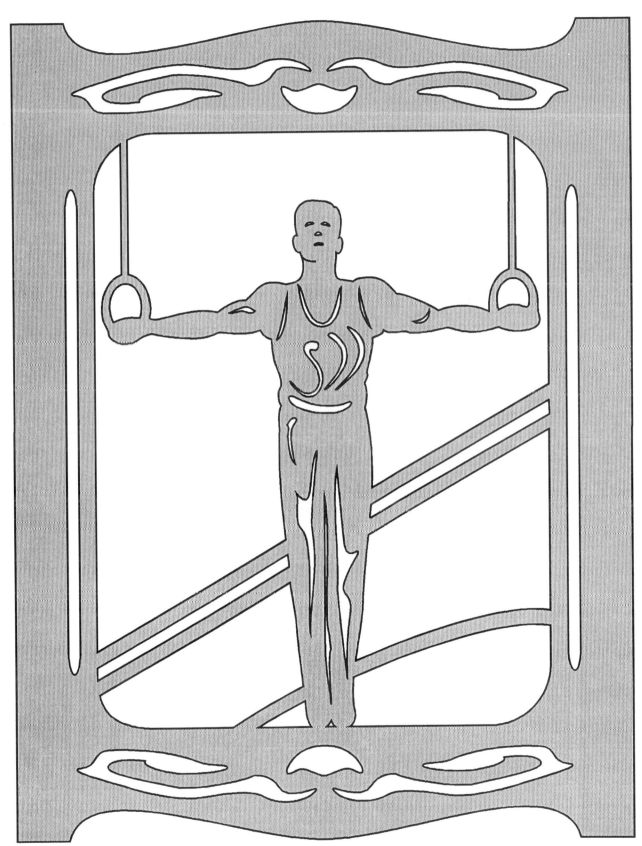

60

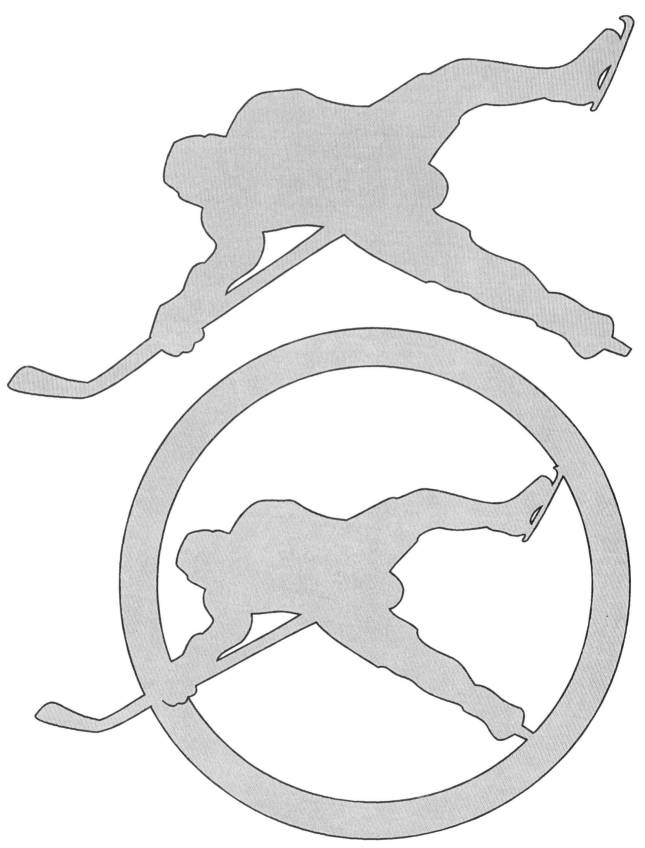

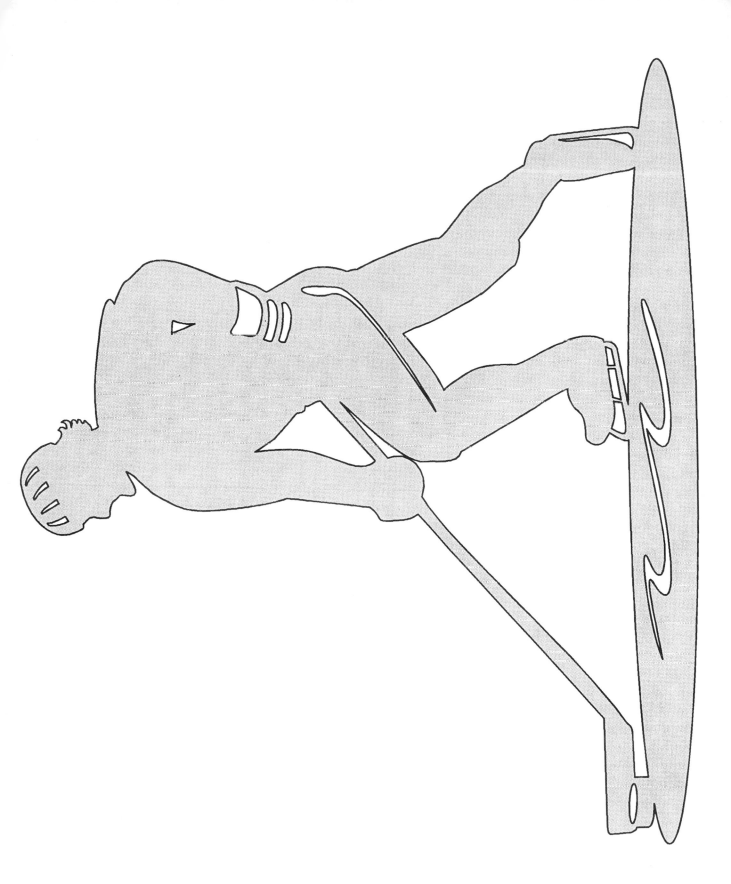

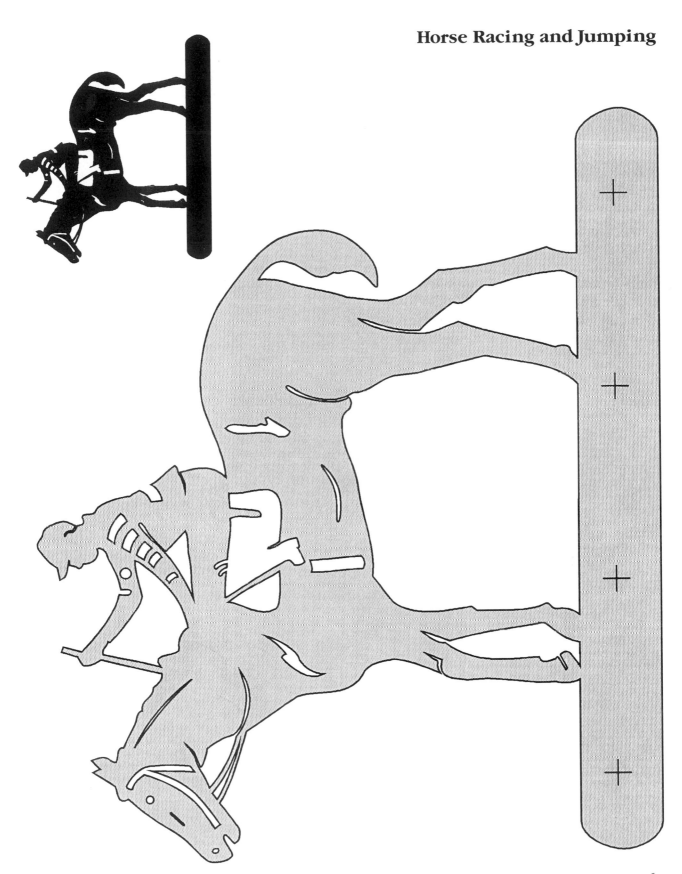

Ice Boating

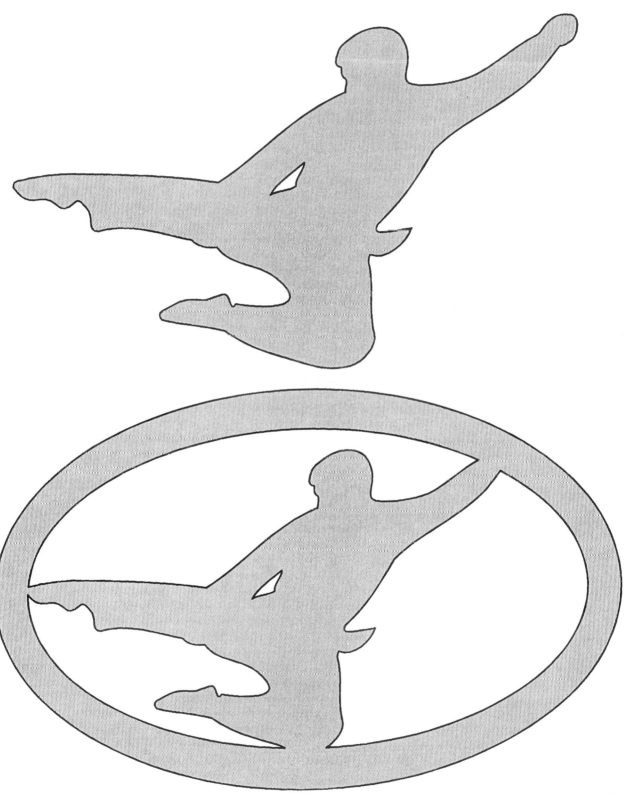

75

Kayaking

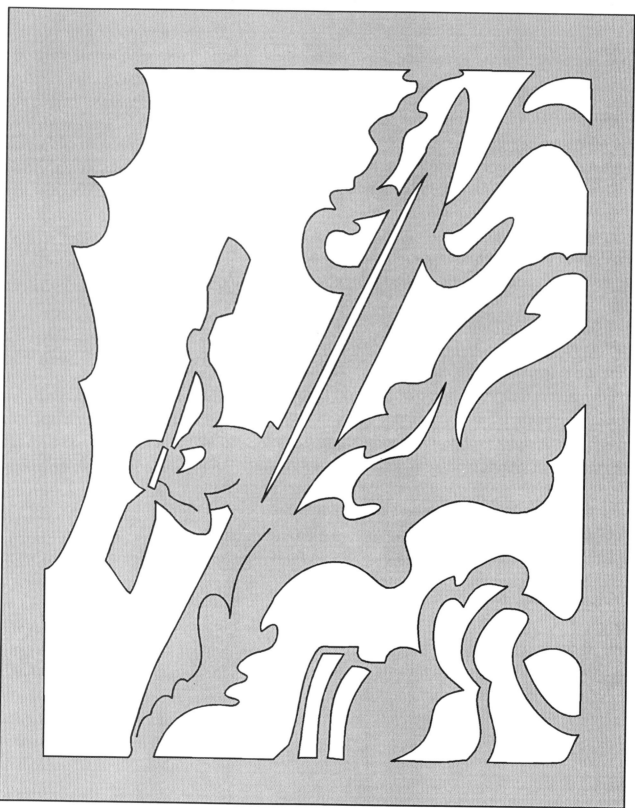

Polo

Skating, Figure

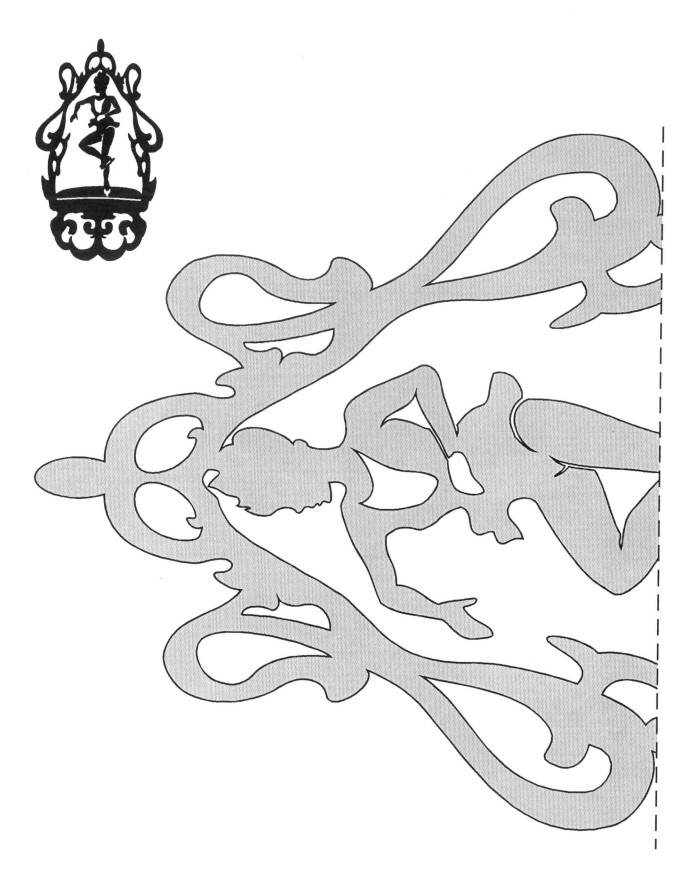

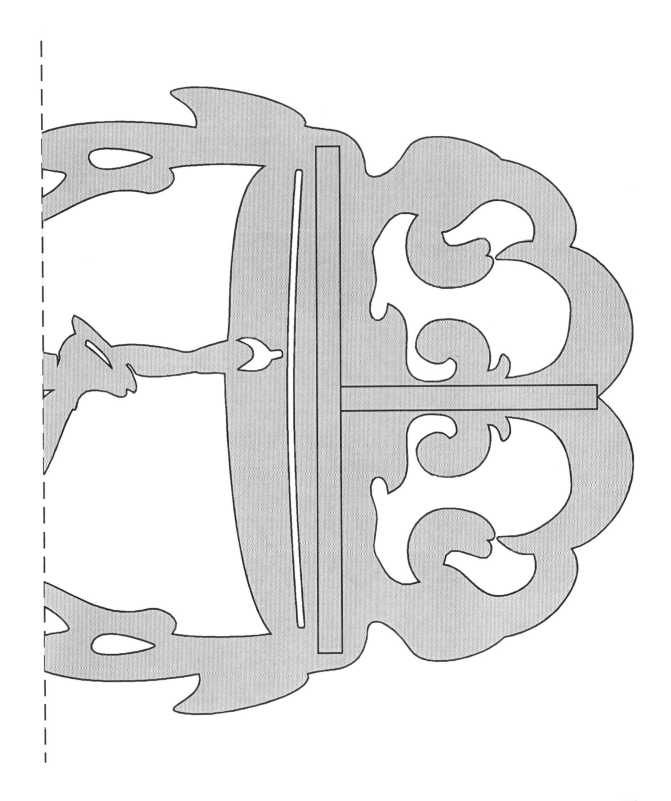

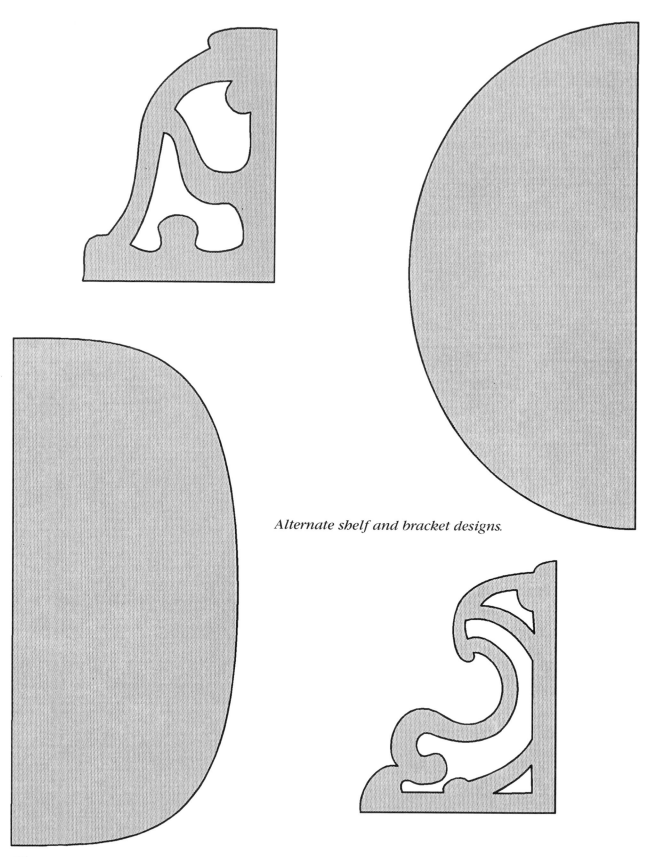

Alternate shelf and bracket designs.

Skating, Speed

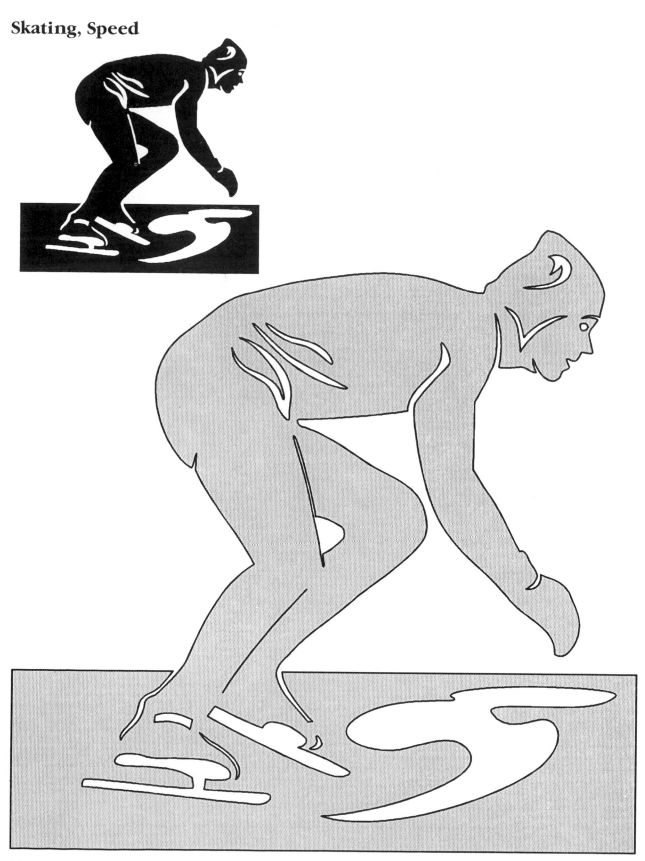

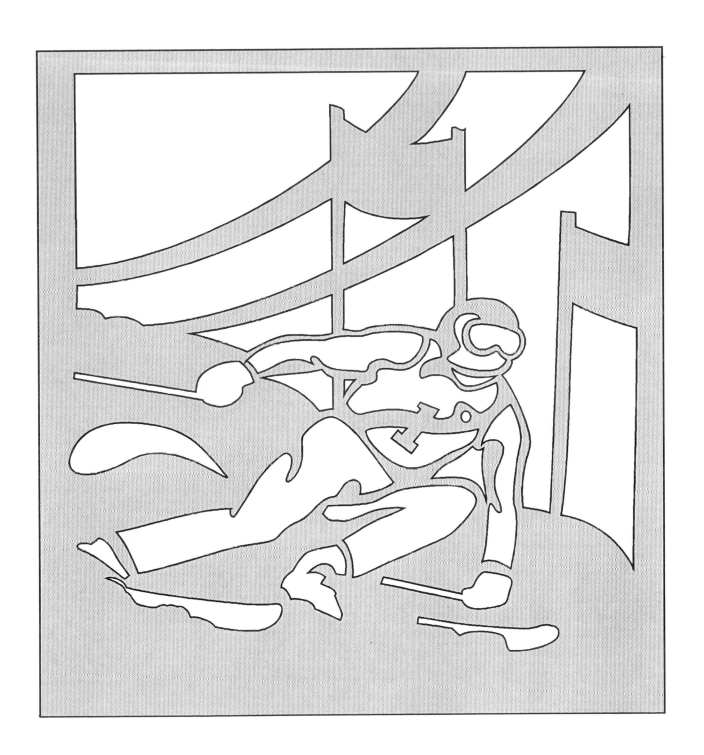

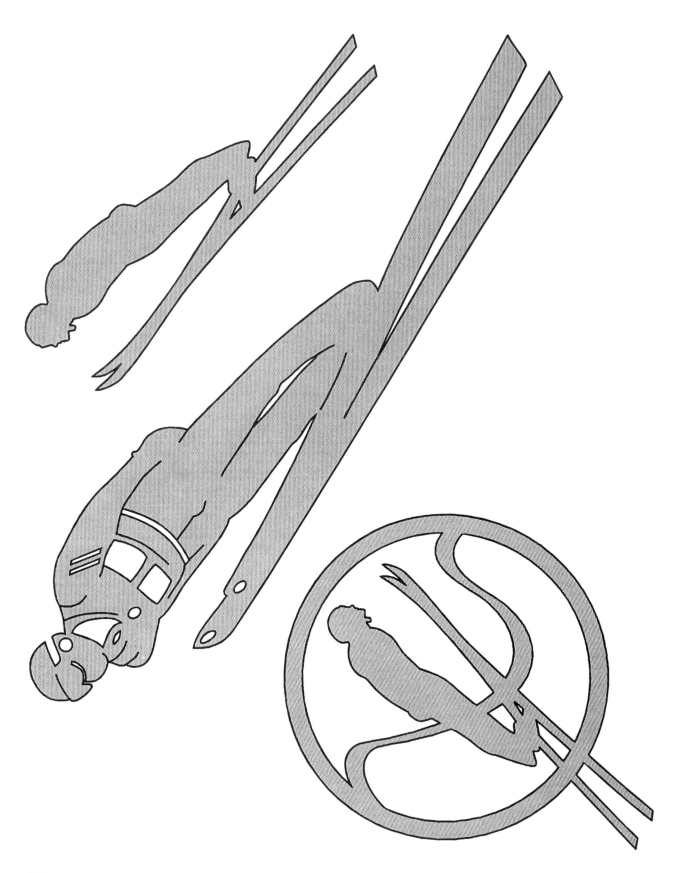

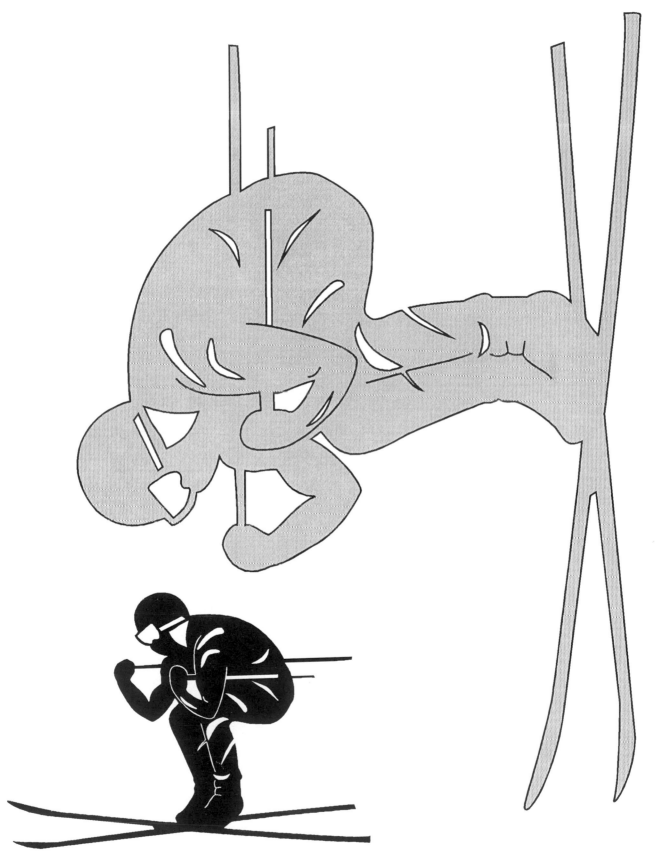

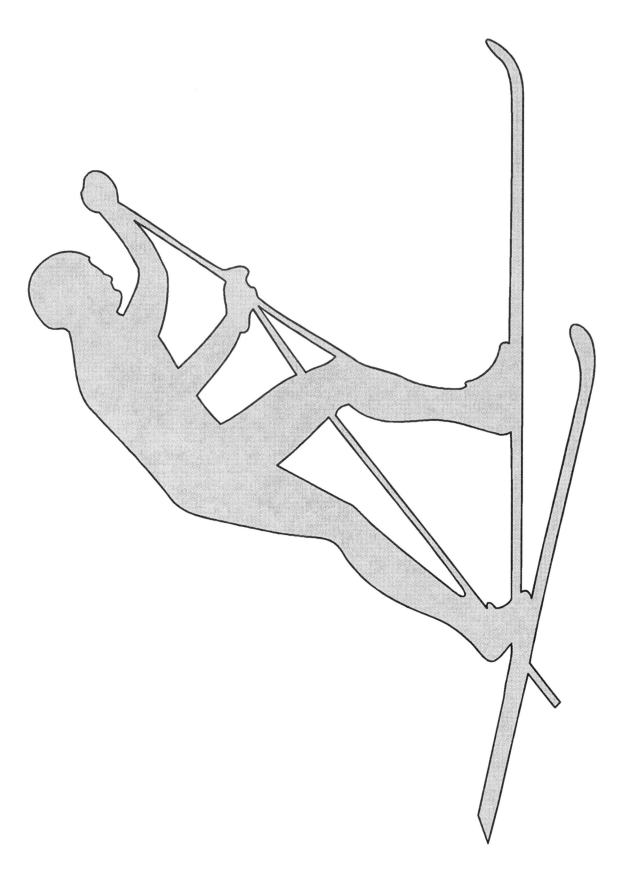

*Cross-country skier key rack cut from ³⁄₈-inch
thick Baltic birch plywood.*

Skin Diving

Soccer

Swimming and Diving

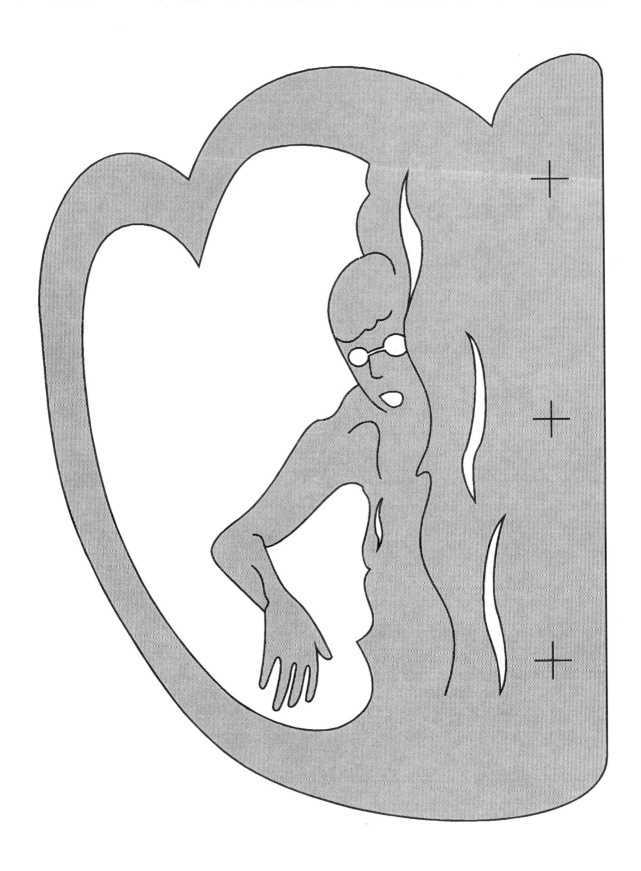

Tennis

A shelf project with an applied overlay.

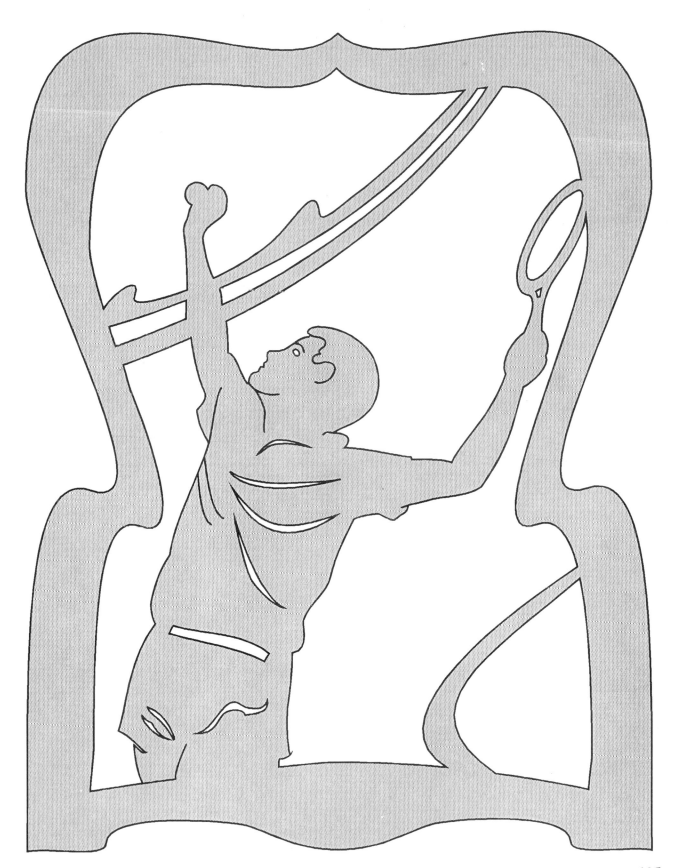

Track and Field, Men

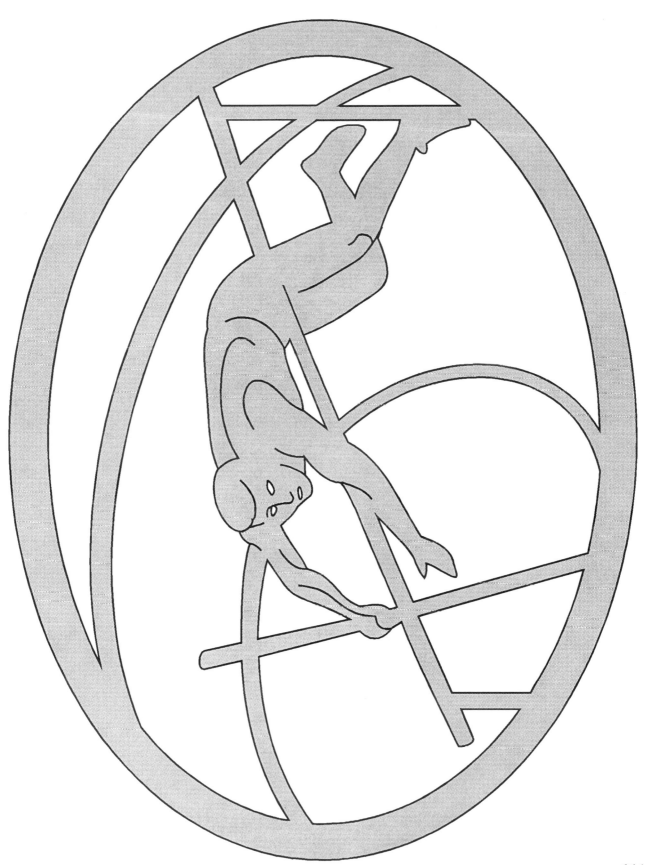

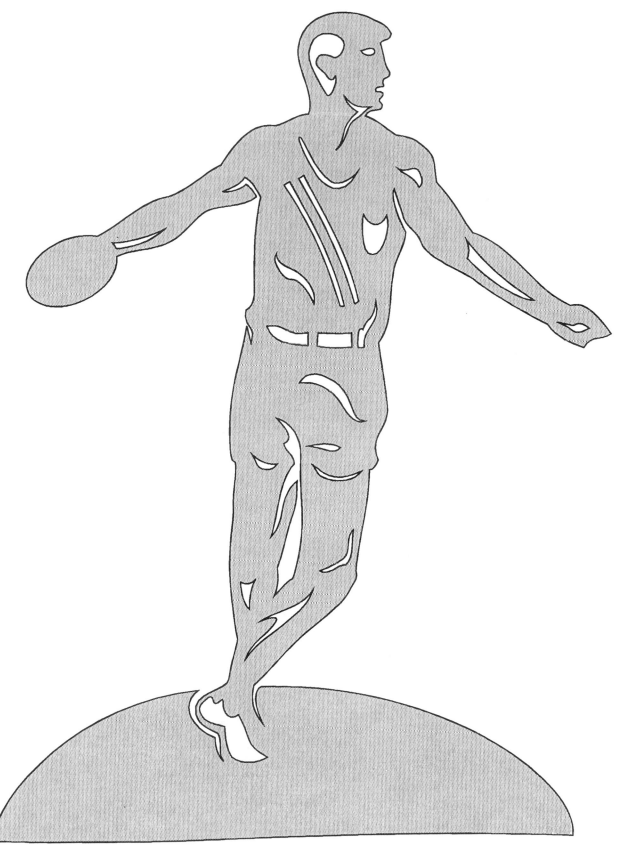

115

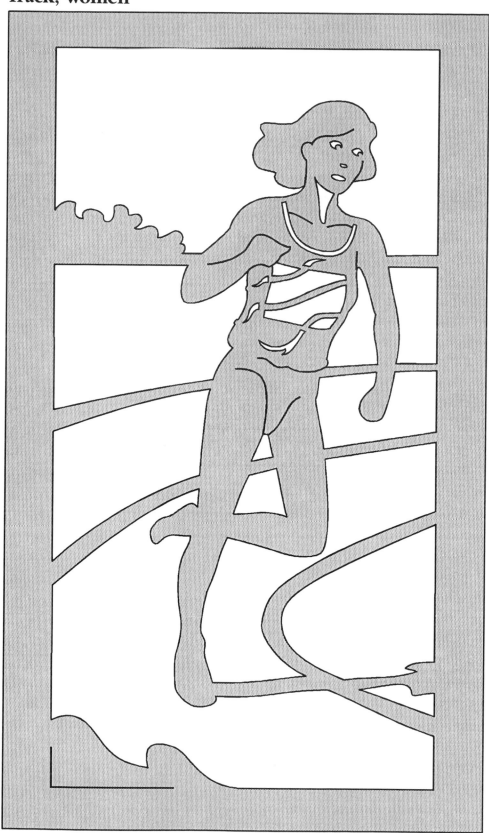

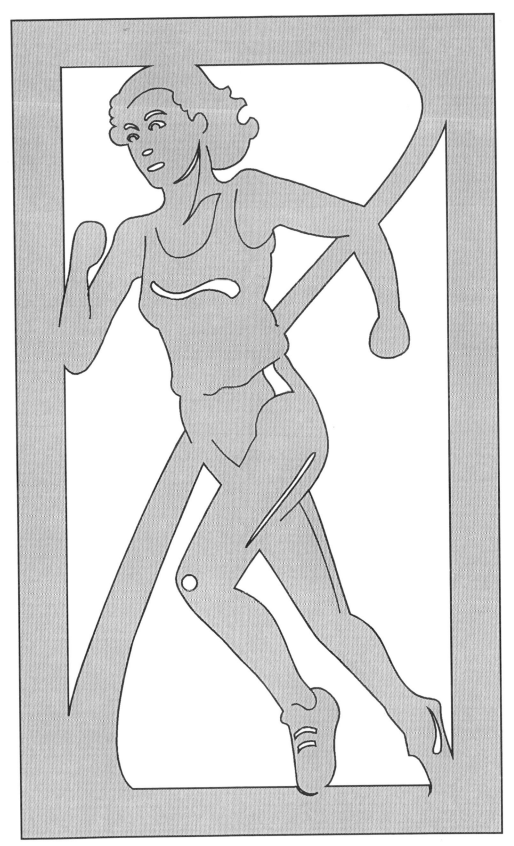

Weight Lifting

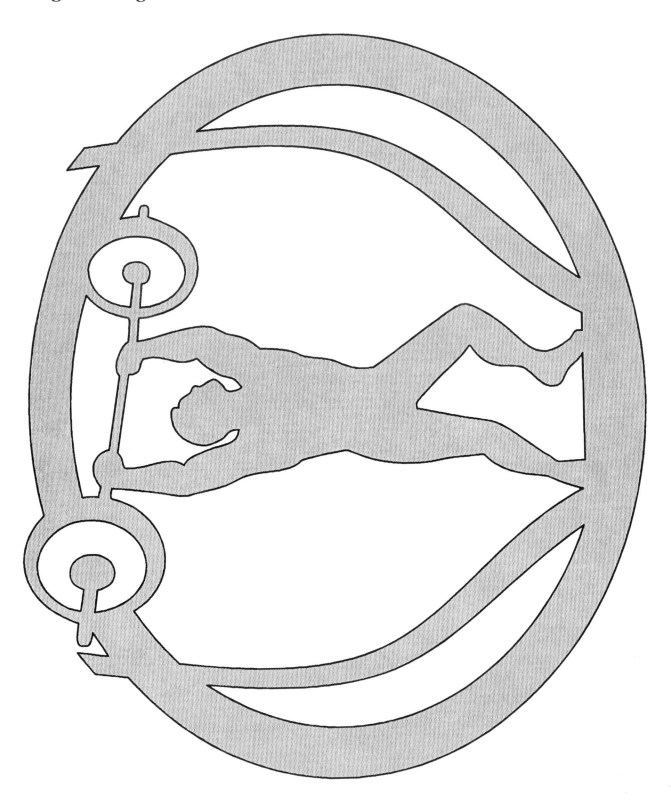

Windsurfing

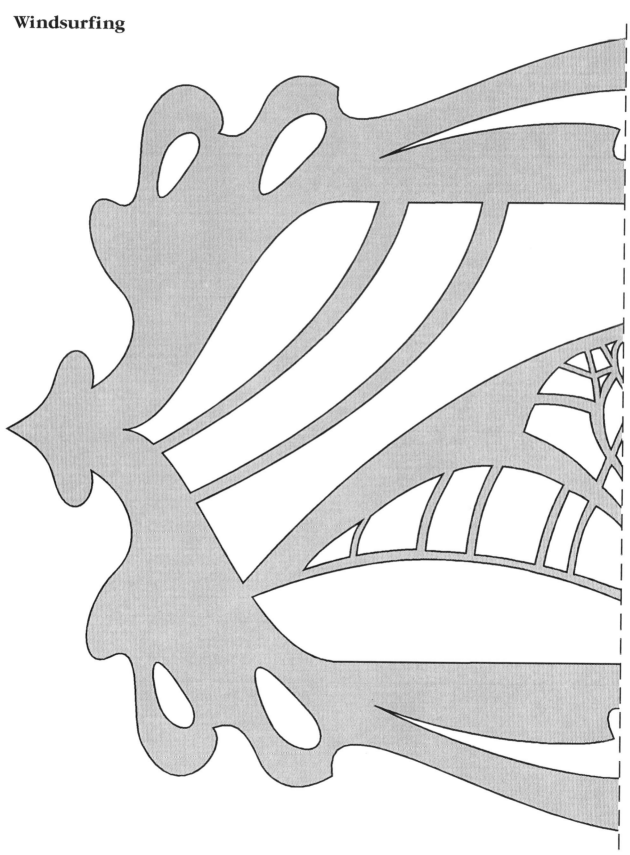

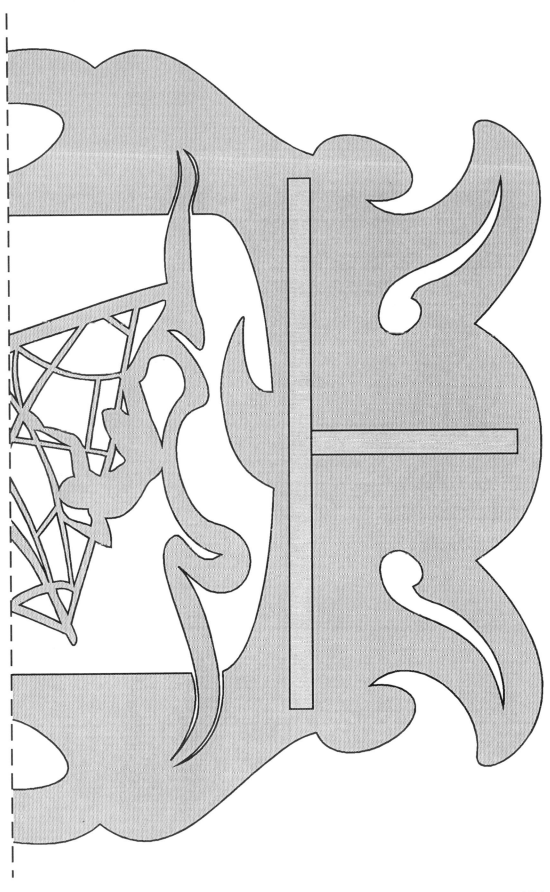

Windsurfing design incorporated into a beautiful wall shelf. Make this project from ¼-inch-thick solid wood (mahogany shown) or use plywood for more strength.

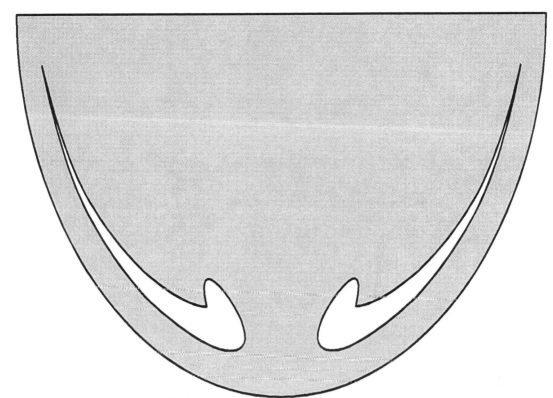

Two different shelf and bracket designs.

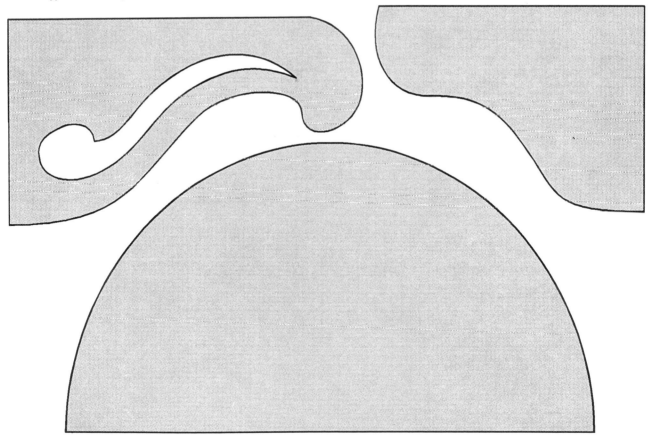

Current Books by Patrick Spielman

Carving Wild Animals: Life-Size Wood Figures. Spielman and renowned woodcarver Bill Dehos show how to carve more than 20 magnificent creatures of the North American wilds. A cougar, black bear, prairie dog, squirrel, raccoon, and fox are some of the life-size animals included. Step-by-step, photo-filled instructions and multiple-view patterns, plus tips on the use of tools, wood selection, finishing, and polishing, help bring each animal to life. Oversized. Over 300 photos. 16 pages in full color. 240 pages.

Christmas Scroll Saw Patterns. Patrick and Patricia Spielman provide over 200 original, full-size scroll saw patterns with Christmas as the theme, including: toys; shelves; tree, window, and table decorations; segmented projects; and alphabets. A wide variety of Santas, trees, and holiday animals are included, as is a short, illustrated review of scroll saw techniques. 4 pages in color. 164 pages.

Classic Fretwork Scroll Saw Patterns. Spielman and coauthor James Reidle provide over 140 imaginative patterns inspired by and derived from mid- to late-19th-century scroll-saw masters. This book covers nearly 30 categories of patterns and includes a brief review of scroll-saw techniques and how to work with patterns. These include ornamental numbers and letters, beautiful birds, signs, wall pockets, silhouettes, a sleigh, jewelry boxes, toy furniture, and more. 192 pages.

Country Mailboxes. Spielman and coauthor Paul Meisel have come up with the 20 best country-style mailbox designs. They include an old pump fire wagon, a Western saddle, a Dalma-tian, and even a boy fishing. Simple instructions cover cutting, painting, decorating, and installation. Over 200 illustrations. 4 pages in color. 164 pages.

Gluing & Clamping. A thorough, up-to-date examination of one of the most critical steps in woodworking. Spielman explores the features of every type of glue—from traditional animal-hide glues to the newest epoxies—the clamps and tools needed, the bonding properties of different wood species, safety tips, and all techniques from edge-to-edge and end-to-end gluing to applying plastic laminates. Also included is a glossary of terms. Over 500 illustrations. 256 pages.

Making Country-Rustic Wood Projects. Hundreds of photos, patterns, and detailed scaled drawings reveal construction methods, woodworking techniques, and Spielman's professional secrets for making indoor and outdoor furniture in the distinctly attractive Country-Rustic style. Covered are all aspects of furniture making from choosing the best wood for the job to texturing smooth boards. Among the dozens of projects are mailboxes, cabinets, shelves, coffee tables, weather vanes, doors, panelling, plant stands, and many other durable and economical pieces. 400 illustrations. 4 pages in color. 164 pages.

Making Wood Bowls with a Router & Scroll Saw. Using scroll-sawn rings, inlays, fretted edges, and much more, Spielman and master craftsman Carl Roehl have developed a completely new approach to creating decorative bowls. Over 200 illustrations. 8 pages in color. 168 pages.

Making Wood Decoys. This clear, step-by-step approach to the basics of decoy carving is abundantly illustrated with close-up photos for designing, selecting, and obtaining woods; tools; feather detailing; painting; and finishing of decorative and working decoys. Six different professional decoy artists are featured. Photo gallery (4 pages in full color) along with numerous detailed plans for various popular decoys. 164 pages.

Making Wood Signs. Designing, selecting woods and tools, and every process through finishing are clearly covered. Instructions for hand and power carving, routing, and sandblasting techniques for small to huge signs. Foolproof guides for professional letters and ornaments. Hundreds of photos (4 pages in full color) Lists sources for supplies and special tooling. 148 pages.

New Router Handbook. This updated and expanded version of the definitive guide to routing continues to revolutionize router use. The text, with over 1,000 illustrations, covers familiar and new routers, bits, accessories, and tables available today; complete maintenance and safety techniques; a multitude of techniques for both hand-held and mounted routers; plus dozens of helpful shop-made fixtures and jigs. 384 pages.

Original Scroll Saw Shelf Patterns. Patrick Spielman and Loren Raty provide over 50 original, full-size patterns for wall shelves, which may be copied applied directly to wood. Photographs of finished shelves are included, as well as information on choosing woods, stack-sawing, and finishing. 4 pages in color. 132 pages.

Realistic Decoys. Spielman and master carver Keith Bridenhagen reveal their successful techniques for carving, feather-texturing, painting, and finishing wood decoys. Details you can't find elsewhere—anatomy, attitudes, markings, and the easy, step-by-step approach to perfect delicate procedures—make this book invaluable. Includes listings for contests, shows, and sources of tools and supplies. 274 close-up photos. 8 pages in color. 232 pages.

Router Basics. With over 200 close-up, step-by-step photos and drawings, this valuable starter handbook will guide the new owner, as well as provide a spark to owners for whom the router isn't the tool they turn to most often. Covers all the basic router styles, along with how-it-works descriptions of all its major features. Includes sections on bits and accessories, as well as square-cutting and trimming, case and furniture routing, cutting circles and arcs, template and freehand routing, and using the router with a router table. 128 pages.

Router Jigs & Techniques. A practical encyclopedia of information, covering the latest equipment to use with the router, it describes all the newest commercial routing machines, along with jigs, bits, and other aids and devices. The book not only provides invaluable tips on how to determine which router and bits to buy, it explains how to get the most out of the equipment once it is bought. Over 800 photos and illustrations. 384 pages.

Scroll Saw Basics. Features more than 275 illustrations covering basic techniques and accessories. Sections include types of saws, features, selection of blades, safety, and how to use patterns. Half a dozen patterns are included to help the scroll saw user get started. Basic cutting techniques are covered, including inside cuts, bevel cuts, stack-sawing, and others. 128 pages.

Scroll Saw Country Patterns. With 300 full-size patterns in 28 categories, this selection of projects covers an extraordinary range, with instructions every step of the way. Projects include farm animals, people, birds, and butterflies, plus letter and key holders, coasters, switch plates, country hearts, and more. Directions for piercing, drilling, sanding, and finishing, as well as tips on using special tools. 4 pages in color. 196 pages.

Scroll Saw Fretwork Patterns. This companion book to *Scroll Saw Fretwork Techniques & Projects* features over 200 fabulous, full-size fretwork patterns. These patterns include popular classic designs, plus an array of imaginative contemporary ones. Choose from a variety of numbers, signs, brackets, animals, miniatures, silhouettes, and more. 256 pages.

Scroll Saw Fretwork Techniques & Projects. A study in the historical development of fretwork, as well as the tools, techniques, materials, and project styles that have evolved over the past 130 years. Every intricate turn and cut is explained, with over 550 step-by-step photos and illustrations. 32 projects are shown in full color. The book also covers some modern scroll-sawing machines as well as state-of-the-art fretwork and fine scroll-sawing techniques. 8 pages in color. 232 pages.

Scroll Saw Handbook. The workshop manual to this versatile tool includes the basics (how scroll saws work, blades to use, etc.) and the advantages and disadvantages of the general types and specific brand-name models on the market. All cutting techniques are detailed, including compound and bevel sawing, making inlays, reliefs, and recesses, cutting metals and other non-woods, and marquetry. There's even a section on transferring patterns to wood. Over 500 illustrations. 256 pages.

Scroll Saw Holiday Patterns. Patrick and Patricia Spielman provide over 100 full-size, shaded patterns for easy cutting, plus full-color photos of projects. Will serve all your holiday pleasures—all year long. Use these holiday patterns to create decorations, centerpieces, mailboxes, and diverse projects to keep or give as gifts. Standard holidays, as well as the four seasons, birthdays, and anniversaries, are represented. 8 pages of color. 168 pages.

Scroll Saw Pattern Book. The original classic pattern book—with over 450 patterns for wall plaques, refrigerator magnets, candle holders, pegboards, jewelry, ornaments, shelves, brackets, picture frames, signboards, and many other projects. Beginning and experienced scroll saw users alike will find something to intrigue and challenge them. 256 pages.

Scroll Saw Patterns for the Country Home. Patrick and Patricia Spielman and Sherri Spielman Valitchka produce a wide-ranging collection of over 200 patterns on country themes, including simple cutouts, mobiles, shelves, sculpture, pull toys, door and window toppers, clock holders, photo frames, layered pictures, and more. Over

80 black-and-white photos and 8 pages of color photos help you to visualize the steps involved as well as the finished projects. General instructions in Spielman's clear and concise style are included. 200 pages.

Scroll Saw Puzzle Patterns. 80 full-size patterns for jigsaw puzzles, stand-up puzzles, and inlay puzzles. With meticulous attention to detail, Patrick and Patricia Spielman provide instructions and step-by-step photos, along with tips on tools and wood selection, for making dinosaurs, camels, hippopotami, alligators—even a family of elephants! Inlay puzzle patterns include basic shapes, numbers, an accurate piece-together map of the United States, and a host of other colorful educational and enjoyable games for children. 8 pages of color. 264 pages.

Scroll Saw Shelf Patterns. Spielman and master scroll saw designer Loren Raty offer full-size patterns for 44 different shelf styles. Designs include wall shelves, corner shelves, and multi-tiered shelves. The patterns work well with ¼-inch hardwood, plywood, or any solid wood. Over 150 illustrations; 4 pages in color. 132 pages.

Scroll Saw Silhouette Patterns. With over 120 designs, Spielman and James Reidle provide an extremely diverse collection of intricate silhouette patterns, ranging from Victorian themes to sports to cowboys. They also include mammals, birds, country and nautical designs, as well as dragons, cars, and Christmas themes. Tips, hints, and advice are included along with detailed photos of finished works. 160 pages.

Sharpening Basics. The ultimate handbook, which goes well beyond the "basics" to become the major up-to-date reference work, features more than 300 detailed illustrations (mostly photos) explaining every facet of tool sharpening. Sections include bench-sharpening tools, sharpening machines, and safety. Chapters cover cleaning tools, and sharpening all sorts of tools, including chisels, plane blades (irons), hand knives, carving tools, turning tools, drill and boring tools, router and shaper tools, jointer and planer knives, drivers and scrapers, and, of course, saws. 128 pages.

Spielman's Original Scroll Saw Patterns. 262 full-size patterns that don't appear elsewhere feature teddy bears, dinosaurs, sports figures, dancers, cowboy cutouts, Christmas ornaments, and dozens more. Fretwork patterns are included for a Viking ship, framed cutouts, wall hangers, key-chain miniatures, jewelry, and much more. Hundreds of step-by-step photos and drawings show how to turn, repeat, and crop each design for thousands of variations. 4 pages of color. 228 pages.

Victorian Gingerbread: Patterns & Techniques. Authentic pattern designs (many full-size) cover the full range of indoor and outdoor detailing: brackets, corbels, shelves, grilles, spandrels, balusters, running trim, headers, valances, gable ornaments, screen doors, pickets, trellises, and much more. Also included are complete plans for Victorian mailboxes, house numbers, signs, and more. With clear instructions and helpful drawings by James Reidle, the book also provides tips for making gingerbread trim. 8 pages in color. 200 pages.

Victorian Scroll Saw Patterns. Intricate original designs plus classics from the 19th century are presented in full-size, shaded patterns. In-structions are provided with drawings and photos. Projects include alphabets and numbers, as well as silhouettes and designs for shelves, frames, filigree baskets, plant holders, decorative boxes, picture frames, welcome signs, architectural ornaments, and much more. 160 pages.

Woodworker's Pattern Library: Alphabets & Numbers. Spielman and daughter Sherri Spielman Valitchka have come up with a collection of 40 alphabets and matching number patterns in the new series the *Woodworker's Pattern Library*. Upper- and lowercase alphabets are presented for all woodworking uses, including block script, italic, and a section on decorative design elements to complement uses of lettering. An introductory section on Basic Tips provides information on enlarging and transferring patterns as well as making templates. 128 pages.

Working Green Wood with PEG. Covers every process for making beautiful, inexpensive projects from green wood without cracking, splitting, or warping it. Hundreds of clear photos and drawings show every step from obtaining the raw wood through shaping, treating, and finishing PEG-treated projects. 175 unusual project ideas. Lists supply sources. 120 pages.

Index